A Woman's JOURNAL

For personal notes & mementos
with women's quotes & illustrations

Edited by Evelyn L. Beilenson
Designed by Michel Design

PETER PAUPER PRESS, INC.
WHITE PLAINS · NEW YORK

For Suzanne Beilenson

Copyright © 1990
Peter Pauper Press, Inc.
202 Mamaroneck Avenue
White Plains, NY 10601
ISBN 0-88088-707-9
Printed in Hong Kong

Dear Diary . .

A journal or diary (the French call it a *journal intime*) is a written account of the day's happenings and reflections. The author keeps this record for a number of reasons.

A nne Frank, one of the 20th Century's best-known diarists, enduring the unendurable, noted in her journal that "I can write down my thoughts and feelings, otherwise I would be absolutely stifled." Virginia Woolf realized that if you don't write down the events of the day, they've "gone down the sink to oblivion." Oscar Wilde amusingly writes in *The Importance of Being Earnest*, that "I never travel without my diary. One should always have something sensational to read on the train."

M ost journals will never be published, however, but are for personal use and enjoyment. *Your* diary may be your best friend, or sometimes even your enemy. Whichever, and for whatever reason, turn the page, write on, and enjoy!

E.L.B.

A woman's virtue is man's greatest invention.

Cornelia Otis Skinner

For most of history, Anonymous was a woman.

Virginia Woolf

*Men are taught to apologize for their
weaknesses, women for their strengths.*

Lois Wyse

You will do foolish things, but
do them with enthusiasm.

Colette

_____

_____

_____

_____

_____

_____

_____

_____

_____

_____

_____

_____

_____

_____

_____

_____

_____

_____

_____

_____

_____

*The trouble with some women is that they
get all excited about nothing—and then
marry him.*

Cher

Women are not forgiven for aging. Bob Redford's
lines of distinction are my old-age wrinkles.

Jane Fonda

Women are the real architects of society.

Harriet Beecher Stowe

The best way to hold a man is in your arms.

Mae West

_____

_____

_____

_____

_____

_____

_____

_____

_____

_____

_____

_____

_____

_____

_____

_____

_____

_____

_____

_____

_____

_____

_____

_____

Pray to God. She will help you.
Alva Vanderbilt Belmont

*I've always believed that one woman's success
can only help another woman's success.*

Gloria Vanderbilt

Woman's place is in the House and in the Senate.

Gloria Schaffer

You grow up the day you have
your first real laugh—at yourself.

Ethel Barrymore

_____

_____

_____

_____

_____

_____

_____

_____

_____

_____

_____

_____

_____

_____

_____

_____

_____

_____

_____

_____

_____

_____

_____

_____

*Money has nothing to do with style at all, but
naturally it helps every situation.*

Diana Vreeland

Our faith in the present dies out long before
our faith in the future.

Ruth Benedict

_____

_____

_____

_____

_____

_____

_____

_____

_____

_____

_____

_____

_____

_____

_____

_____

_____

_____

_____

_____

"We, the people of the United States." Which
"We, the people"? The women were not included.

Lucy Stone

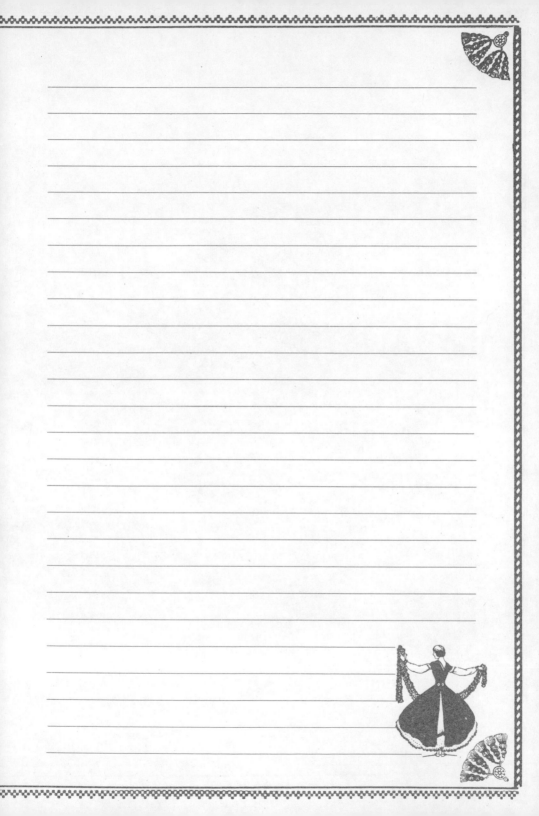

_The prerequisite for making love is to like
someone enormously._

Helen Gurley Brown

There is no hope even that woman, with her
right to vote, will ever purify politics.

Emma Goldman

Now, we are becoming the men we wanted to marry. Once women were trained to marry a doctor, not be one.

Gloria Steinem

_____

_____

_____

_____

_____

_____

_____

_____

_____

_____

_____

_____

_____

_____

_____

_____

_____

_____

_____

_____

You can't be too rich or too thin.
Wallis Simpson, Duchess of Windsor

Adventure is worthwhile in itself.

Amelia Earhart

*One cannot be always laughing at a man
without now and then stumbling on
something witty.*

Jane Austen

I like to wake up feeling a new man.

Jean Harlow

Husbands are like fires. They go out if unattended.

Zsa Zsa Gabor

_____

_____

_____

_____

_____

_____

_____

_____

_____

_____

_____

_____

_____

_____

_____

_____

_____

_____

_____

_____

_____

_____

_____

I never hated a man enough to give him
his diamonds back.

Zsa Zsa Gabor

It is always incomprehensible to a man that a woman should refuse an offer of marriage.

Jane Austen

*A husband is what is left of the lover after
the nerve has been extracted.*

Helen Rowland

Beware of the man who praises women's
liberation; he is about to quit his job.

Erica Jong

_____

_____

_____

_____

_____

_____

_____

_____

_____

_____

_____

_____

_____

_____

_____

_____

_____

_____

_____

_____

_____

_____

_____

_____

_____

When a girl marries she exchanges the attentions
of many men for the inattention of one.

Helen Rowland

One is not born a woman, one becomes one.

Simone de Beauvoir

I never loved a man I liked—and never
liked a man I loved.

Fanny Brice

_____

_____

_____

_____

_____

_____

_____

_____

_____

_____

_____

_____

_____

_____

_____

_____

_____

_____

_____

_____

_____

_____

_____

If a man watches three football games in a row, he should be declared legally dead.

Erma Bombeck

*The secret of staying young is to live
honestly, eat slowly, and lie about your age.*

Lucille Ball

_____

_____

_____

_____

_____

_____

_____

_____

_____

_____

_____

_____

_____

_____

_____

_____

_____

_____

_____

_____

_____

_____

_____

_____

Love, the quest; marriage, the conquest;
divorce, the inquest.

Helen Rowland

Love is an archer with a low I.Q.

Phyllis McGinley

_____

_____

_____

_____

_____

_____

_____

_____

_____

_____

_____

_____

_____

_____

_____

_____

_____

_____

_____

_____

_____

_____

_____

I have everything I had twenty years ago,
only it's all a little bit lower.

Gypsy Rose Lee

I've never been lifted. But I do like a bit of glamour in the morning.

Louise Nevelson

*I cannot and will not cut my conscience to fit
this year's fashions.*

Lillian Hellman

Just remember, we're all in this alone.

Lily Tomlin

The delights of self-discovery are always available.

Gail Sheehy

Brevity is the soul of lingerie.

Dorothy Parker

It's better to light a candle than to curse the darkness.

Eleanor Roosevelt

_____

_____

_____

_____

_____

_____

_____

_____

_____

_____

_____

_____

_____

_____

_____

_____

_____

_____

_____

_____

_____

_____

_____

Sure, I'm for helping the elderly. I'm going to
be old myself someday.

Lillian Carter

Sometimes when I look at all my children, I say to myself,
"Lillian, you should have stayed a virgin."

Lillian Carter

I'm having trouble managing the mansion.
What I need is a wife.

Governor Ella T. Grasso

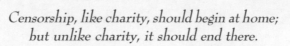

Censorship, like charity, should begin at home;
but unlike charity, it should end there.

Clare Boothe Luce

_____

_____

_____

_____

_____

_____

_____

_____

_____

_____

_____

_____

_____

_____

_____

_____

_____

_____

_____

_____

_____

_____

_____

The true republic—men, their rights and nothing more;
women, their rights and nothing less.

Susan B. Anthony

_____

_____

_____

_____

_____

_____

_____

_____

_____

_____

_____

_____

_____

_____

_____

_____

_____

_____

_____

_____

_____

_____

_I think you can destroy your now by
worrying about tomorrow._

Janis Joplin

Man forgives woman anything save
the wit to outwit him.

Minna Antrim

Growing old gracefully sure beats dying with dignity.

Martha Holland Bartsch

---

*No matter how many communes anybody
invents, the family always creeps back.*

Margaret Mead